# KINDERGARTEN READY

## THROUGH PLAY

75+ Play-Based Learning Activities for Toddlers & Preschoolers

Becca Gasiewicz Thiemann, PhD
& Sarah Liebenrood, MEd

# DEDICATION

For our sweet children who love to play, read, and keep us on
our toes. Your love for learning inspired this book and ignited
our passion for literacy.

We are also grateful to our kind, patient,
and supportive husbands.
Thank you for encouraging us every step of the way.

# TABLE OF CONTENTS

# TABLE OF CONTENTS

# TABLE OF CONTENTS

# TABLE OF CONTENTS

# TABLE OF CONTENTS

# INTRODUCTION

# ALL ABOUT BECCA & SARAH

Becca and Sarah are both moms and educators with a passion for helping parents and teachers create lifelong readers!

### BECCA GASIEWICZ THIEMANN
### PHD IN LITERACY

Becca has over 13 years of experience as a classroom teacher, university instructor, and tutor. She owns a tutoring business in Cincinnati that serves students and families in a variety of ways. Becca loves sharing her love of kids and literacy on her social media pages! You can reach out about tutoring through her webpage, Becca's Book Box & Tutoring Services.

### SARAH LIEBENROOD
### MED IN LITERACY

Sarah has over 13 years of experience as a classroom teacher and instructional coach. She is currently taking time away from the school setting to stay home with her two children and tutor local students. She loves sharing her passion with literacy through her website, Wonderfully Read, and on her social media pages.

# HOW TO USE THIS BOOK

The MOST important thing to remember is that a LOVE of learning is key to academic success. Our goal is to help you engage with your child in a way that gets them excited about LEARNING and PLAY!

"Good development requires patience and faith. The problem with pushing and controlling is they can interfere with providing what children really need. They can create stressful environments where children feel there is something wrong with the way they are."
- Deborah MacNamara, Rest Play Grow

## Follow Your Child's Lead

Children develop at different paces and are ready at different times. Some children will be ready for a lot of these activities at the age of two or three, and others will not be ready until after four.  If you a try an activity and it doesn't go over well or they are not interested, please do not get frustrated or give up. They may love that activity next month!  When they are showing interest, engage with them, and when they are resisting, do not force it.

## Don't Compare

Every single child is on a different journey and progressing at a different pace - developmentally, academically, and emotionally.  Whether it is a sibling, a peer, or parental perception, avoid comparison at all cost.  It does not help growth and only puts undue pressure on your child and you.

## Keep it Simple

Use the supplies you have around the house! You don't need all the new flashy learning toys. Books, Post-It notes, blocks, favorite toys, and stickers can all provide fun and valuable learning experiences. You do NOT need to do an activity everyday or even close to everyday. Use the activities shared here when you need something fresh and new!

## Don't Wait Until Kindergarten to Start

Think about what your child can do or what they might be interested in and start there. Toddlers LOVE books with rhyming, painting, and play invitations. We have done a majority of these activities with our own children, who are ages two through five!

# HAVE FUN & PLAY!

# WHY KINDERGARTEN READY THROUGH PLAY?

When a child enters kindergarten with the developmentally appropriate foundations, they are more likely to have success throughout their academic career. With a focus on kindergarten readiness, many schools and parents feel that using flashcards and test prep materials to prepare their children is the most effective way. The research shows that the most developmentally appropriate way for children to learn is through **PLAY**. In fact, "The single most significant factor influencing a child's early educational success is an introduction to books and being read to at home prior to the beginning of school" (National Commission on Reading). Preparing children for kindergarten can be fun, simple,
and provide a foundation for a lifelong love
of reading and learning.

**Our goal is to share that PLAY IS LEARNING and an imperative part of childhood and preparing for school.**

"Children learn best through first-hand experiences—play motivates, stimulates and supports children in their development of skills, concepts, language acquisition, communication skills, and concentration."

(O'Leary 2021)

# TEN TIPS FOR PARENTS

1. Every child's "readiness" for school will look different and that is OKAY!

2. All focus should be on play and learning will come through play.

3. Follow your child's lead with learning. If they show interest, spend time with them and feed their curiosities.

4. Use your child's interests to to guide the learning. If they love trucks, read all about trucks. If they love ballet, read all about ballet.

5. Time spent reading makes a HUGE difference.

6. Allow your child to play and explore the items (blocks, magnatiles, etc) BEFORE you begin the activity. This will help them stay focused on the activity and may even inspire some different play ideas!

7. Let children grow at their own pace. Provide a safe space full of love and children will flourish knowing they have the space to be themselves.

8. Communication is SO important. Once your child begins preschool our kindergarten, Do not be afraid to ask your child's teacher questions and be open to suggestions.

9. Instead of asking your child "How was your day?" Ask specific question like:
   - What made you laugh today?
   - What made you smile today?
   - Did anything upset you today?

10. Once your child enters kindergarten, continue playing and learning with them.

Reading 20 minutes a day exposes kids to 1.8 MILLION words per year.

# F.A.Q.S

## HOW MANY SOUNDS SHOULD MY CHILD KNOW BEFORE KINDERGARTEN?

Before kindergarten, children do not need to know every single letter and sound, but a solid foundation of letters will help them as readers. Using the letters in their name and letters that are important to them is a great place to start!

## HOW OFTEN SHOULD I READ WITH MY CHILD?

Before kindergarten and for many years after, children should be read to and with for at least 20 minutes per day. It does not have to be 20 straight minutes - you can break it up throughout the day!

## WHAT DO I DO IF MY CHILD CONFUSES LETTERS WHEN READING & WRITING?

Reversing letters can be very common until about age 8. When working with similar letters at home (like b/d or q/p) try to only introduce one letter at a time, allow for repetition, and use multisensory ways to practice the letters.

## WHAT ARE THE BEST BOOKS TO READ WITH MY CHILD?

Any books they are interested in! Children at this age LOVE to make a choice on what, where, when or how they are reading. This is the perfect time to let them take charge or take them to the library to introduce new books!

## HOW CAN I HELP MY CHILD WITH EARLY LITERACY SKILLS?

In kindergarten, children should recognize rhyming words and create rhyming pairs, such as cat/mat. They can practice identifying the beginning and ending sounds in a word and tell you how many sounds are in a word (cat = c-a-t = 3 sounds).

> "The developing brain triples in the first year alone and is virtually fully formed by the time a child enters kindergarten."
>
> (Eliot, 1999)

# F.A.Q.S

## WHAT ORDER SHOULD I TEACH MY CHILD THE LETTERS?

Before kindergarten, children do not need to know every single letter and sound but a solid foundation of letters will help them as readers. Using the letters in their name and letters that are important to them is a great place to start!

## SO MY CHILD KNOWS THE ABC SONG, NOW WHAT?

Songs are a great place to start with learning. Most kids love them and enjoy singing them. With alphabet learning, the next step would be to begin with their name. Research has been inconclusive about the right letter order to teach, but it has concluded that beginning with their name is the best place to start!

## DO I NEED TO DO THESE ACTIVITIES EVERY DAY?

No! The most important things you can do for your child is read with them, provide opportunities for play, and talk with your child every day. If you have time or need something fun to do, we love these activities!

## WHAT IF MY CHILD HAS NO INTEREST IN READING OR LEARNING WITH ME?

Children are ready to learn and engage at different times. The more you push, the more they will resist. Focus on play and allow the learning to happen through play.

## WHAT IS SCHOOL READINESS?

School readiness can be defined generally as the skills, knowledge, and abilities that children need to succeed in formal schooling, which, for most, begins at kindergarten (Snow, 2006).

> "How much fathers talk to young children has a direct positive effect on their early academic achievement."
>
> Baker, Vernon-Feagans, & the Family Life Project Investigators, 2015

# OUR FAVORITE SUPPLIES

💡 **TIP**

USE WHAT YOU HAVE AT HOME:
- QTIPS
- PAPER TOWEL ROLLS
- COOKIE SHEET
- SHAVING CREAM
- MEASURING CUPS
- CARDBOARD BOXES

# PLAY

### What is play?

Play is "what children and young people do when they follow their own ideas, in their own way and for their own reasons" (Lester & Russell, 2008). In other words, play in the uninhibited time children are allowed to use their own creativity and imagination to engage in activities of their choosing.

### Why is play important?

Play is the most valuable use of children's time. Children MUST play and spend lots of open-ended time doing so. This section provides some fun ways to invite children into play.

### Keep in mind...

- "No one has ever watched a child intent in his play without being made aware of the complete merging of playfulness and seriousness" (Cuffaro, 1995).
- "What play may do is help children to be better children, rather than help them prepare to be adults" (Lester & Russell, 2008).

> "Play is one of the most important ways in which young children gain essential knowledge and skills."
>
> Learning Through Play, 2018

# 6 STAGES OF PLAY

## UNOCCUPIED PLAY - BIRTH TO 3 MONTHS

- Infants begin to play by moving their arms, legs, hands and feet.
- These movements are random and allow the baby to explore their new environment.

## SOLITARY PLAY - BIRTH TO 2 YEARS

- Children play alone and do not typically interact with other children.
- They play with their own toys independently.

## SPECTATOR/ONLOOKER PLAY - BIRTH TO 2 YEARS

- Children just watch and observe other children at play.

## PARALLEL PLAY - 2.5 TO 3.5 YEARS

- Children begin to play side by side by not interacting. Even though they are not interacting, they are still aware of the other children.
- Children may begin to copy what the other children are doing.

## ASSOCIATIVE PLAY - 3 TO 4.5 YEARS

- Children begin to interact with one another while they are playing.
- They may ask questions and talk about the toys they are playing with.
- This sets the foundation for getting along with other children.

## SOCIAL/COOPERATIVE PLAY - 4+ YEARS

- Children are playing together to accomplish a common goal.
- At this stage, children begin taking turns and understanding how to work together.

# TYPES OF PLAY

## DRAMATIC/FANTASY PLAY

This is better known as "make believe" play. Dramatic and fantasy play allow children to create their own worlds and rules and then play within those limits. This is the best place for kids to learn self-control!

## CONNECTED PLAY

Making connections for kids is helpful. They may see a parent using tools at a tool bench, but sharing books and puzzles that make those connections give kids a context for play. Follow their interests and create a play invitation like this one!

## PHYSICAL PLAY

Physical play encourages children to enjoy being active, develop fitness skills and develop their gross and motor skills. This type of play can be anything from small movements (throwing a ball, picking up a rock) to large movements (running and jumping).

## CONSTRUCTIVE/BUILDING PLAY

Blocks, ball tracks, car tracks, trains, and more are all examples of building and creating. Children want to test their abilities. They have an inner desire to experiment and see what they can do. **Provide materials to build, create, and imagine!**

# TYPES OF PLAY

## COMPETITIVE PLAY

Children begin to learn that some types of play (like games) have rules, require turn taking and being a part of a team.

## PRACTICAL LIFE

One of the things we love most about the Montessori philosophy is the idea that children need practical life experiences. We may look at these things as chores and work, but children often love the chance to participate in these parts of life.

## OUTDOOR PLAY

Open, unstructured, outdoor play is critical for kids. In our over-scheduled world, kids MUST have time to play without limits. Prioritize that time. Allow them to get wet, dirty, experiment, and PLAY!

## SENSORY PLAY

Sensory play is a great opportunity for children to play while developing their senses. Children use their senses to play and make sense of the world around them.

Play is essential to healthy human functioning, especially for development in the early years because it is (1) where the self is truly expressed, (2) where growth and development take play, and (3) where psychological health and well-being are preserved.
(MacNamara, 2016)

# PLAY INVITATIONS

## WHAT IS A PLAY INVITATION?

A play invitation is an open-ended play set up for children to explore and to foster independent play by setting their toys up in new and inviting ways. A play invitation can include toys, art supplies, or household items. Play invitations are a great way to spark a child's imagination .

## HOW DO I SET UP A PLAY INVITATION?

A play invitation can be as simple or as elaborate as you want it to be! Sometimes a cardboard box and crayons is more than enough to spark some creativity and engage your child in play for hours!

To set up a play invitation, think about the items you already own and your child's interest. We use books to inspire play all the time. We have provided on the next few pages some play invitation ideas paired with books to help you get started.

## HOW OFTEN DO I SET UP A PLAY INVITATION?

You can use a play invitation or set up when you need it. It's not something we do every day, and many times, the same play invitation will be played with for days or weeks at a time. Think of a play invitation as a play reset. When your children are having trouble engaging in independent play, this is a great time to setup a play invitation.

**TIP** SO MANY OF OUR PLAY INVITATIONS ARE INSPIRED BY BOOKS THAT OUR CHILDREN LOVE AND WANT TO READ OVER AND OVER AGAIN!

# PIZZA PIZZA!

## MATERIALS TO USE:

- Play Pizza Set
- Pizza Theme Book
- If you don't own a pizza set, use felt to make your own.

## THE SET UP:

Set the book out with the pizza set. Allow the child to explore the pizza set and create their own pizza. They can take your pizza order, pretend to bake it and enjoy a delicious play pizza.

 TIP THINK ABOUT WHAT YOUR CHILD LOVES MOST. CREATE A PLAY INVITATION THAT BRINGS THAT TOGETHER!

# KIDS LOVE TACOS!

## MATERIALS TO USE:

- Dragons Love Tacos
- Dragons Love Tacos 2
- Construction Paper
- Tissue Paper
- Pom Poms
- Mini Kitchen Tongs
- Felt

## THE SET UP:

Use construction paper, felts, and tissue paper to create the ingredients. In the picture above we used:

- tortilla shell - felt circle
- meat - crumpled construction paper
- lettuce -  folded green construction paper
- tomatos - pom poms
- cheese - felt pieces

Set up the taco bar so they can create their own tacos!

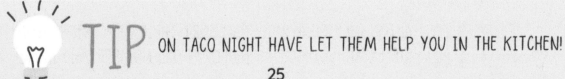

**TIP** ON TACO NIGHT HAVE LET THEM HELP YOU IN THE KITCHEN!

# LET'S GO SHOPPING

## MATERIALS TO USE:

- toys that children are interested in
- Books
- Puzzles

## THE SET UP:

Using items from the kitchen or toys to set up this fun practical life play invitation. Allow children to explore books to inspire play!

 TIP AFTER THEY SHOP THEY CAN SORT THEIR GROCERIES INTO DIFFERENT CATEGORIES (COLOR, TYPE, NUMBER AND MORE!)

# TEA TIME

## MATERIALS TO USE:

- Tea Set
- Stuffed Animals
- Tea Party Books

## THE SET UP:

Set up a fun tea party with their favorite stuffed animals, siblings, or friends! Place pretend food, tea cups, and tea pot with place settings to encourage play. Children can practice life skills like taking turns and table manners while they play!

**TIP** A PLASTIC TEA SET IS PERFECT FOR AN OUTDOOR PICNIC OR TEA PARTY.

# DOWN ON THE FARM

## MATERIALS TO USE:

- Farm books
- Tractor toys
- Farm figurine animals
- Farm puzzle

## THE SET UP:

Invite children to create and interact with the farm by setting up an open area to play with farm vehicles and animals. Allow them to pretend to be the farmer or the animals. When they seem to disengage, read the farm books to reignite their imagination!

 **TIP** FOR TODDLERS, THIS IS A GREAT WAY TO TEACH ANIMAL SOUNDS!

# ICE CREAM SHOP

## MATERIALS TO USE:

- Ice Cream Toys (Play Dough is a great alternative)
- Sprinkles
- Empty Chocolate Syrup Bottle
- Ice Cream Theme Books

## THE SET UP:

I scream, you scream, all the kids want ice cream! Set up an ice cream station for you kids to create their favorite ice cream flavors. Kids can serve each other or have an ice cream party!

 **TIP** AFTER READING & PLAYING, TAKE A TRIP TO THE REAL ICE CREAM STORE TO MAKE A REAL WORLD CONNECTION.

# LET'S BUILD

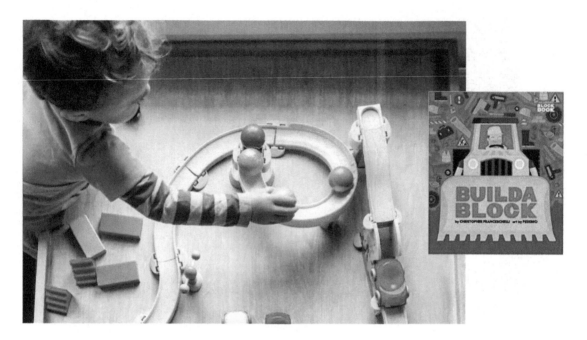

## MATERIALS TO USE:

- train set
- legos
- magnatiles
- wooden blocks
- plastic blocks

## THE SET UP:

Blocks, ball tracks, car tracks, trains, and more are all examples of building and creating. Children want to test their abilities. They have an inner desire to experiment and see what they can do. **Provide materials to build, create, and imagine!**

TIP ASK YOUR CHILD TO DESCRIBE WHAT THEY ARE BUILDING AND HOW IT WILL WORK.

# WORKING ON THE RAILROAD

## MATERIALS TO USE:

- train tracks
- train cars
- train stories
- non-fiction books about trains

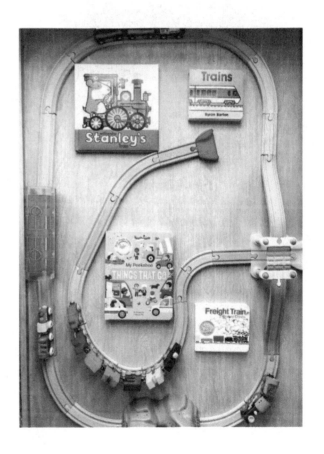

## THE SET UP:

Beginning at the age of two, it is important for children to be able to see cause and effect as well as track the movements of an item. Trains are a perfect opportunity to practice these skills and experiment with movement and tracking.

 TIP KIDS NEED TO TAKE RISKS. GUIDE THEM CAREFULLY THROUGH THE RISK VERSUS NOT ALLOWING IT.

# A BUGGY WORLD!

## MATERIALS TO USE:

- insect themed books
- toob animals
- magnifying glass
- net for real bugs
- shovel to dig for bugs

## THE SET UP:

Children are very curious especially about nature and the world we live in! During the spring and summer insects are out and ready to be discovered. Creating a sensory bin to learn about bugs or going on a bug hunt is a great way to connect with nature.

TIP CHILDREN CAN SORT THE INSECTS INTO CATEGORIES (EXAMPLE: FLY OR CRAWL).

# CAR WASH

## MATERIALS TO USE:

- plastic container
- toy cars
- liquid soap
- sponges/brushes

## THE SET UP:

Kids LOVE going through the car wash and their toys probably need a good scrub! Fill a plastic tub with warm water and add some dish soap. Grab some toy cars and let the kids wash away!

Don't forget a towel for drying!

 **TIP** SET UP A CAR WASH FOR THE KIDS TO WASH YOUR REAL CARS!

# WE BUILT THIS CITY

## MATERIALS TO USE:

- Wooden Town Playset
- Town Theme Books

## THE SET UP:

Use a wooden block town set and begin to start building the town. Allow the child to continue building, moving buildings, cars and trees around to create their own special town. Use Lego or figurines to add people and animals to the town.

## TIP

USE A CARDBOARD BOX TO SET UP THE TOWN TO DRAW ROADS.

# CLIMBING HIGH

## MATERIALS TO USE:

- playground equipment
- balls
- bike
- any sporting equipment

## THE SET UP:

Physical play encourages children to enjoy being active, develop fitness skills and develop their gross and motor skills. This type of play can be anything from small movements (throwing a ball, picking up a rock) to large movements (running and jumping).

TIP KIDS NEED TO TAKE RISKS. GUIDE THEM CAREFULLY THROUC THE RISK VERSUS NOT ALLOWING IT.

35

# LET'S GET SHOVELING!

## MATERIALS TO USE:

- plants
- cleaning supplies
- yard tools
- kitchen utensils

## THE SET UP:

One of the things we love most about the Montessori philosophy is the idea that children need practical life experiences. We may look at these things as chores and work, but children often love the chance to participate in these parts of life.

TIP INCLUDE YOUR CHILD IN CHORES - LAUNDRY, SWEEPING, DUSTING, WATERING. THEY LOVE IT!

# WASHING THE DISHES

## MATERIALS TO USE:

- cleaning supplies
- sink (real or toy)
- kitchen utensils

## THE SET UP

Kids want to do what they see you doing. Anything they can play with that is similar to your every day life is appealing and interesting to them. This sink is a perfect example of something kids love because it actually works and it's water and fun!

 TIP THINK OF WAYS TO CREATE PLAY SIMILAR TO WHAT THEY SEE YOU DOING! THEY JUST WANT TO BE LIKE YOU!

# ADVENTURE WALK

## MATERIALS TO USE:

- The Great Outdoors!
- Dirt
- Flowers
- Rainboots
- Sunscreen

## THE SET UP:

Open, unstructured, outdoor play is critical for kids. In our over-scheduled world, kids MUST have time to play without limits. Prioritize that time. Allow them to get wet, dirty, experiment, and PLAY!

 TIP OUTDOOR LOOSE PARTS ARE THE BEST - THINK STICKS, ROCKS, SAND, LEAVES, TUBES, ANYTHING!

# FRUIT PUNCH

## MATERIALS TO USE:

- plastic fruit
- Fruit Theme Book
- mixing bowl with water
- plastic cups
- ladle
- towel/plastic mat*

## THE SET UP:

Fill mixing bowl with water and place in plastic bin. Place some of the fruit in the mixing bowl with the ladle. Place a few plastic cups next to the mixing bowl. Kids can create their own fruit punch and serve it up!

*Putting a shower liner, splat mat, or towel under the play set up to help contain the mess!

**TIP** READ "MRS. PEANUCKLE'S FRUIT ALPHABET" BOOK WHILE THEY ENJOY THEIR "FRUIT PUNCH!"

# STOP AND SMELL THE ROSES

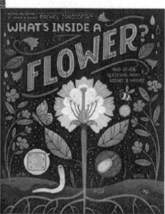

## MATERIALS TO USE:

- The Great Outdoors!
- Dirt
- Flowers
- Rain boots
- Sunscreen

## THE SET UP:

Allow your child the space to choose to do what they want to do. Remember, this play and space does NOT need toys but rather things they find outdoors, conversation about what they are seeing, and books to support their learning.

 TIP TRY TO THINK WHAT YOU CAN PUT IN YOUR YARD THAT CAN BE HANDS ON FOR YOUR CHILD.

# FLOWER SENSORY BIN

## MATERIALS TO USE:

- Bin to hold materials
- TOOB Flower Figurines
- Dry Black Beans
- Spray Bottle
- Plastic Flower Pots
- Shovel/Garden Tools

## THE SET UP:

Sensory Bins are a great way to allow your children to explore. Place flower and gardening objects together in dry black beans and allow your child to plant and water flowers. BONUS - The water bottle builds hand strength!

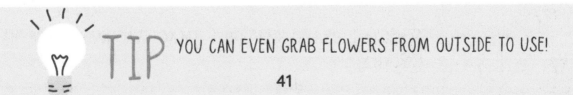

TIP YOU CAN EVEN GRAB FLOWERS FROM OUTSIDE TO USE!

# LET'S GO TO THE BEACH

## MATERIALS TO USE:

- Kinetic Sand
- Water
- Food Coloring
- Sand Toys
- Ocean Animal Figurines
- Large Plastic Tub
- Small Plastic Tub

## THE SET UP:

Bring the beach home! Add kinetic sand in a large storage container and then place the smaller tub inside filled with water and a few drops of food coloring. Add sand toys, ocean animal figurines and watch your child explore the wonderful world of the beach!

 TIP SENSORY BINS CAN HELP BUILD BACKGROUND KNOWLEDGE AND EXPERIENCES.

# TISSUE PAPER ART PLAY

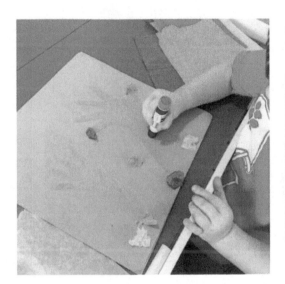 

## MATERIALS TO USE:

- Tissue Paper
- Glue
- Contact Paper (or construction paper)

## THE SET UP:

Using tissue paper to create art is a fun and beautiful way to bring a child's creativity to life! Use tissue paper to place eon contact paper to create objects (hearts, flowers, sun, cloud, moons, etc). or crumple them up to create leaves or other scenes.

 TIP BALLING UP THE TISSUE PAPER IS A GREAT FINE MOTOR ACTIVITY TO BUILD HAND STRENGTH.

43

# CUT IT OUT!

## MATERIALS TO USE:

- tissue paper
- yarn
- post it notes
- construction paper
- straws
- preschool scissors

## THE SET UP:

Scissor skills are in important fine motor skill that children will need and use in kindergarten. "We Are Growing" by Laurie Keller is a fun read to pair with this activity. Place different types of materials in a bin and give the child freedom to cut, play and create!

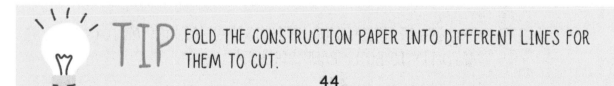

TIP FOLD THE CONSTRUCTION PAPER INTO DIFFERENT LINES FOR THEM TO CUT.

# LET IT SNOW!

## MATERIALS TO USE:

- contact paper
- painter's tape
- construction paper cutouts
- white pompoms
- books about snow

## THE SET UP:

Using painter's tape, tape contact paper to the window, sticky side out. Have a model showing and then allow your child to create their own. Resist the urge to intervene when they are creating. Leave it up for a while so they can admire their hard work!

TIP  THINK OF WAYS TO CREATE PLAY SIMILAR TO WHAT THEY SEE YOU DOING! THEY JUST WANT TO BE LIKE YOU!

45

# PLAY ON THE GO

## LITERACY BUSY BAG

A Literacy Busy Bag is an on-the-go bag filled with a few activities to keep your child busy and learning while waiting. I recommend having 3-4 small activities in the bag with at least one book. This way, no matter how long the wait, you're able to keep your child happy and busy!

## BENEFITS OF A LITERACY BUSY BAG

- It will keep your child entertained so going out to eat with little kids is more enjoyable!
- Build literacy skills that are developmentally appropriate for your specific child.
- Fosters independence and creativity while on the go!

## ACTIVITIES FOR A LITERACY BUSY BAG

- Small Books
- Magnetic Letters
- Play dough
- Wipe Clean Books
- Blank Books with Crayons
- Dot Stickers
- Magnatiles

TIP THINK OF WAYS TO CREATE PLAY SIMILAR TO WHAT THEY SEE YOU DOING! THEY JUST WANT TO BE LIKE YOU!

# MORE PLAY ON THE GO

Think about what you child is interested in most and create a fun bag on that topic. Just like a play invitation, this bag should invite them play and explore while they wait. Here are some ideas!

## TRUCK BAG

- Fiction and non-fiction books about trucks
- Two trucks to interact
- Moving pieces to play with and manipulate.

## PIZZA BAG

- Fiction and non-fiction books about pizza
- A pizza to make and create
- Moving pieces to play with and manipulate.

 TIP — THE BUSY BAG ONLY COMES OUT WHEN YOU ARE WAITING SOMEWHERE SO THE TOYS AND BOOKS ARE FRESH AND ENGAGING!

# MORE PLAY ON THE GO

Creating a car basket for those trips around town or longer road trips can be super helpful to keep kids playing instead of asking, "Are we there yet?!?"

## CAR KIT IDEAS:

- Interactive Books
- Wipe Clean Books
- baggie of figurines
- play dough
- legos
- cookie sheet with lego plate
- stickers
- coloring Pages
- small bag of favorite toys
- Fruit Loops with yarn to make a necklace snack

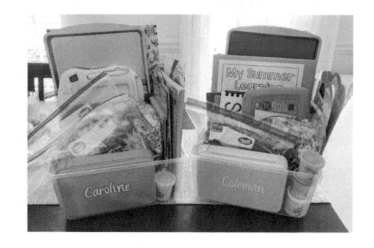

 **TIP** USE A COOKIE SHEET AS A PLAY AREA AND IT CAN DOUBLE FOR A FOOD TRAY!

# READING

# BEST BOOKS FOR STARTING KINDERGARTEN

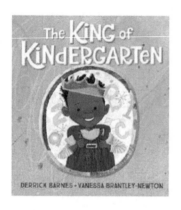

# OTHER BOOK RECOMMENDATIONS

## FOR PARENTS

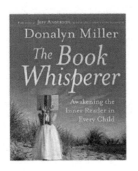   

## FOR KIDS

  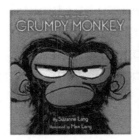 

   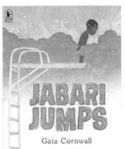

# READING

## What should reading look like for toddlers and preschoolers?

- The goal is for reading to begin at a young age, be a consistent part of their daily life, and be a positive and fun experience.
- Often parents have a vision of a child sitting on their lap or next to them and listening quietly. Shift your thinking to include movement, play, and reading a various times like the breakfast table or the bathtub.

## Why is reading important?

- Extensive research has been done that shows the immense impact reading has on speech, vocabulary, communication, comprehension, and more.
- It lays the academic foundation and instills a love of learning early on.

## Keep in Mind...

- Although the goal is to read at least 20 minutes a day, some days it will hopefully be more, and some days will be less.
- It may look different than you anticipate and that is OKAY!

> Creating a steady stream of new, age-appropriate books has been shown to nearly triple interest in reading within months.
> (Harris, 2003)

# PRINT AWARENESS

## MATERIALS TO USE:

- Books
- Magazines
- Other items with print - cereal boxes, games, puzzles, etc.

## DESCRIPTION:

Print awareness is the idea that letters have sounds and make up words, words make up sentences and what we read, and the concept of how a book works - reading left to right and front to back.

## INTRODUCTION:

- Model orienting the book, turning the pages, and point out things as you read.
- As your child demonstrates an understanding of book concepts, you can point to words as you say them, follow your reading with your finger, allow them to engage by turning pages and pointing things out.

 TIP THIS DOES NOT NEED TO BE FOCUSED AND DIRECTED BUT SHOULD BE A NATURAL PART OF YOUR READING.

# READING FOR 20 MINUTES

## MATERIALS TO USE:

- Any reading material
- Books the child selects

## DESCRIPTION:

Research has shown that reading can have a positive impact as early as 30 weeks gestation. Begin reading early and make a positive part of your day. Reading regularly is a habit we want to instill early but we should think outside the box on when we read - for example, in the car, at quiet time, and before bed.

## INTRODUCTION:

- Think of it like the treadmill. If you are out of shape, you can't hop on and run at a good clip for 20 minutes. Start small and work your way up.
- Make it a priority just like sport's practice.
- Read WITH your child. Either read to them, next to them, or at least to get them started.

**TIP** CHILDREN FOLLOW YOUR LEAD AND YOU ARE THEIR MODEL. UTILIZE THAT POWER!

# BOOK CHOICE

## MATERIALS TO USE:

- Library books
- Books from home

## DESCRIPTION:

Children want to be in control. The best way to engage them is to allow them the autonomy to pick the book, even if you have read it again and again. Use your child's interests to purchase or borrow books that would likely interest them.

## INTRODUCTION:

- Place books strategically around the house - in their play space, in their bedroom, at the breakfast table, next to the potty, wherever!
- Display some books in a forward-facing manner to allow the characters and cover of the books to invite your reader.
- Rotate books regularly to enhance engagement.

**TIP** HEARING A BOOK 300 TIMES HAS HUGE BENEFITS - VOCABULARY, LANGUAGE, COMPREHENSION, AND MORE!

# INVITING A CHILD TO READ

## MATERIALS TO USE:

- Cozy area to read
- Undivided attention
- Engaging books

## DESCRIPTION:

Think of inviting a child to read like you would invite a friend to a party. You want to convey enthusiasm and that you really want them to be there! Use and engaging books and excited to voice to pull them into the story. Allow that time to be special and undivided. Make it something you both look forward to!

## INTRODUCTION:

- It not likely your child will initiate the reading. You will likely need to sit down in their space, grab a book, and start reading for them to join you.
- You can introduce a book by asking a question about the front cover or pointing out something you like about the book.

 **TIP** YOUR CHILD DOES NOT NEED TO SIT STILL FOR READING. READ TO THEM WHILE THEY BUILD, PLAY, AND EAT!

# BACKGROUND KNOWLEDGE

## MATERIALS TO USE:

- Book cover
- Book jacket
- Illustrations

## DESCRIPTION:

In order for children to understand and comprehend what they are reading, they need a context in which to place the knowledge. Find out what knowledge they have related to the book by asking questions like - Do you see anything familiar? What does this book remind you of? What do you know about *topic*?

## INTRODUCTION:

- Browse the illustrations together before reading
- This is a great way to start conversation but do NOT force it. Quizzing and questioning can really disengage some children.
- Allow the child the space to talk and tell what they know.

💡 **TIP** AS YOU READ, ALLOW YOUR CHILD TO POINT THINGS OUT THAT THEY CONNECT WITH AND KNOW!

# BOOK PLACEMENT AT HOME

## MATERIALS TO USE:

- Baskets - all different sizes
- Bookshelves
- Forward-facing shelves

## DESCRIPTION:

A child's engagement in reading is often dictated by the availability of books. Research has shown that book placement, vast amounts of books, and reading in the home has a direct and positive effect on academic achievement. Strategically place books in locations where the child spends time and frequently rotate the books available in each location.

## INTRODUCTION:

Show the child the books in the basket, tell them the topic or theme, and show them how to return the books when they are done. Spend time looking at the books and read anytime they request you to do so.

 TIP THE BREAKFAST TABLE IS A MAGICAL PLACE TO PUT A SMALL BASKET OF BOOKS.

# BOOK PLACEMENT AT HOME

BREAKFAST
BOOK BASKET

SEASONAL
BOOK BASKET

CAR
BOOK BASKET

SHELVES AT
KID HEIGHT

FORWARD
FACING

PAIRED
WITH PLAY

 TIP    ROTATING THESE TOPICS AND BASKETS REGULARLY IS KEY!

# VOCABULARY

## MATERIALS TO USE:

- High-interest books
- Repeatedly read books

## DESCRIPTION:

If a child reads 20 minutes a day, they are exposed to 1.8 million words a year! Imagine what that does for vocabulary. Aim for words they will hear if different contexts, such as, tangled, chilly, patient, hammock, etc.

## INTRODUCTION:

- When your child is really interested in a particular topic or you have read a favorite book again and again, that is the time to ask about new words.
- Ask if there is a word they are unsure of and use the pictures and the context to show them.

TIP KIDS LOVE TO LEARN NEW THINGS, SO THIS IS A GREAT WAY TO ADD INTEREST TO A FAVORITE LOVED BOOK!

# COMPREHENSION QUESTIONS

## MATERIALS TO USE:

- Any reading material they are interested in
- New books

## DESCRIPTION:

The key here is to avoid quizzing and and focus on genuine conversation. Let the child focus on what they are curious about and follow their lead. You do not always have to ask a question, but instead share what you are thinking and noticing. Kids do best with modeling. Be that model reader.

## INTRODUCTION:

- The first few times you ask a question, your child may not be able to or want to answer. Allow time for them to answer and then model how you would answer the question.
- Give lots of space for your child to ask the questions too!

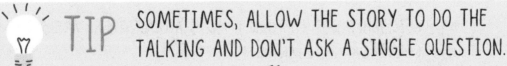

TIP SOMETIMES, ALLOW THE STORY TO DO THE TALKING AND DON'T ASK A SINGLE QUESTION.

# QUESTION EXAMPLES

## COMPREHENSION TALKING POINTS:

- I noticed the character _____. What do you think about that?
- Wow! I see something in the pictures that I didn't hear about when I was reading. Do you see what I am talking about?
- How do you think the character is feeling right now? Why do you think so?
- I feel like the story is about to get exciting. Do you think so?
- This story takes place _____. Would you want to visit there?
- Would you want to be friends with the character? Why?
- Does the character remind you of anyone? Who? What is similar?
- Do you know what _____(new word) means? How can we figure it out together?
- We learned so much about _____. What else do you want to learn?
- I loved the part of the story when _____. What was your favorite part?

TIP REMEMBER NOT TO TURN IT INTO A QUIZ. THESE ARE JUST CONVERSATION STARTERS!

# SETTING THE PACE

## MATERIALS TO USE:

- Reading materials

## DESCRIPTION:

As parents, we are used to setting the pace for our children. We challenge you to allow your child to set the pace for reading. Turn the page turning over to them. Give them the time to look at the pictures and ask questions. If they want to go back in the story, that is okay too. This is the beginning of turning ownership of the reading process over to them.

## INTRODUCTION:

- Tell your child that they are in charge of turning the pages. They get to decide how long they look at pictures and they can ask questions.
- If they decide to change books in the middle of the story, that is okay too.

TIP THE MORE YOU ALLOW THEM TO SET THE PACE, THE BETTER THEY WILL BECOME AT IT.

# MAINTAINING THE HABIT

## MATERIALS TO USE:

- Reading materials
- Family calendar

## DESCRIPTION:

Like anything, the key is to maintaining the habit. The best way to do that is to make reading time something everyone looks forward to. Our goal should be to treat reading like a treat and not a chore. Make it a fun part of your family and then it will not be hard to maintain.

## INTRODUCTION:

- When you are focusing on building the habit, try things like Family Reading Night or going for a drive and listening to an audiobook.
- At first, you will have to dedicate time to read WITH and TO your child to build that reading stamina.
- Don't give up even if you are out of the habit for a while!

TIP TAKE TIME TO FIGURE OUT WHAT WORKS BEST FOR YOUR FAMILY AND STICK TO IT.

LETTER
KNOWLEDGE

# LETTER KNOWLEDGE

### What is letter knowledge?

Letter knowledge is the ability to recognize and name the letters and their corresponding sounds.

### Why is letter knowledge important?

As children gain an understanding that words have meaning, letters make up words, and letters have corresponding sounds, it is important we provide them (not force them) with the opportunity to learn these letter sounds and names.

### Keep in mind...

- Some letters represent multiple sounds.
- Sometimes two letters represent the same sound (think c and k).

> Children's knowledge of letter names and sounds is the best predictor of their later reading and spelling abilities.
> (Hammill, 2004)

# BEST BOOKS FOR
# LETTER KNOWLEDGE

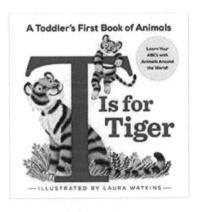

# STICKER MAP

## MATERIALS TO USE:

- Construction Paper
- Markers
- Sticker Collection Book

## DIRECTIONS:

1. Choose a letter to teach the name and sound.
2. Place stickers in the circle map that begin with the same letter sound.
3. Create a circle map for each letter to put together an ABC Book.

## MODIFICATIONS:

- To extend the activity your child could begin to find words that begin with digraphs (th, sh, ch) or blends (br, cr, dr, tr) and other initial sounds.
- Children can begin to write each word underneath the sticker.

 TIP YOU CAN USE STICKERS, TOYS OR PICTURES TO CREATE A CIRCLE MAP OF THE SOUND.

# I SPY OUTSIDE...

## MATERIALS TO USE:

- Anything outside or inside!
- Binoculars (not necessary but FUN!)

## DIRECTIONS:

1. Choose an object that you see outside. Say, "I spy outside something that begins with the /f/ sound!"
2. Have your child guess what the object could be!

## MODIFICATIONS:

- You can play this game anywhere!
- If the item is something they can collect - use sidewalk chalk to write the letter beside the item!

 **TIP** THIS IS A FUN GAME TO PLAY WHILE IN THE CAR OR ON A WALK!

# STICKER MAGNATILES

## MATERIALS TO USE:

- Magnatiles
- Dry Eraser Marker
- Sticker Collection Book
- Cookie Sheet (optional)

## DIRECTIONS:

1. Write a letter on the triangle shaped Magnatile ("roof") with a dry erase marker.
2. Add stickers to the square or rectangle shaped Magnatile that begins with the letter sound.

## MODIFICATIONS:

- Have the little learner write the letter on the triangle "roof" after they have identified the sound and letter.

 TIP  MAGNETIC TILES WILL STICK TO THE FRIDGE, GARAGE DOOR OR A COOKIE SHEET!

# PICTURE SORT

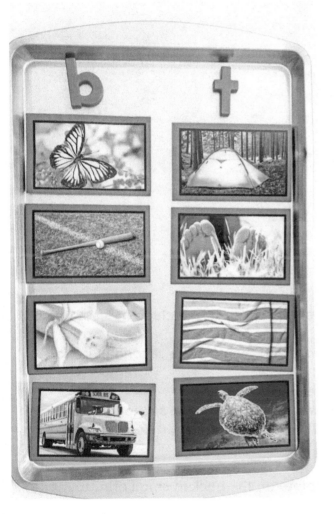

## MATERIALS TO USE:

- Magnetic Letters
- Picture Cards
- Cookie Sheet (optional)

## DIRECTIONS:

1. Choose two letters that your child is learning and place those letters at the top of your workspace (cookie sheet/paper, etc)
2. Using picture cards (or other items) have the child say the name of the picture and then decide which column it belongs in.

## MODIFICATIONS:

- Before adding the magnetic letter to the top of each column, have your child identify the sound and letter.

 TIP AVOID SORTING LETTERS THAT HAVE SIMILAR SOUNDS.

# PAPER PLATE PUZZLE

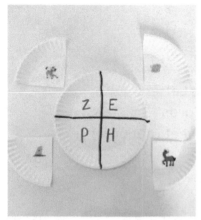 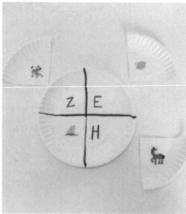 

## MATERIALS TO USE:

- 2 Paper Plates (or construction paper)
- Markers/Scissors
- Sticker Collection Book

## DIRECTIONS:

1. Choose between 2 and 4 letter sounds to practice. Tip: Include at least one short vowel.
2. Draw the outline on the first paper plate and then cut the second plate to match the lines.
3. Write each letter on the section of the plate.
4. Using a sticker book (or you can draw it if you don't have stickers) add a picture that matches the letter sounds.

## MODIFICATIONS:

- Add the correct sound on the sticker plate on the back in small print to make it self checking.
- You can extend the activity to include sight words, blends, digraphs, and more!

 **TIP** ALLOW YOUR CHILD TO WRITE THE LETTER USING A MARKER OF CHOICE TO PRACTICE LETTER FORMATION.

# LETTER MATCH

## MATERIALS TO USE:

- Paper Towel Roll
- Sharpie Marker
- Dot Stickers

## DIRECTIONS:

1. Write the letters of the alphabet on a paper towel roll and then on the dot stickers.
2. Place the stickers to match the corresponding letter on the paper towel roll.

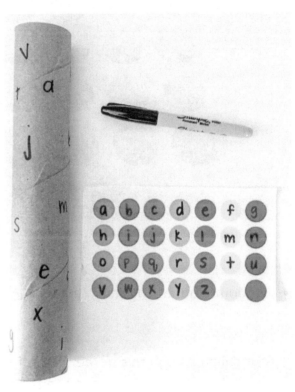

## MODIFICATIONS:

- To extend the activity your child could begin to find words that begin with digraphs (th, sh, ch) or blends (br, cr, dr, tr) and other initial sounds.
- Children can begin to write each word underneath the sticker.

 TIP IF YOU DON'T HAVE A PAPER TOWEL ROLL, YOU CAN WRITE THE LETTERS ON A PIECE OF PAPER. IT'S ALSO GREAT FINE MOTOR PRACTICE!

# GONE FISHING!

## MATERIALS TO USE:

- Coogam Magnetic Fishing Game (Available at Walmart & Amazon)

## DIRECTIONS:

1. Your child can use this game to fish for letters. They can say the name and sound the letter makes when they "catch" it.
2. You can extend the learning by asking for a word that begins with that letter.

## MODIFICATIONS:

- You can ask your child to go "fishing" for a specific letter.
- Ask your child to find the letter that represents the /p/ sound as in pole.

TIP    USE THE FISH TO PRACTICE SPELLING YOUR CHILD'S NAME.

# LABEL THE BOOKS

## MATERIALS TO USE:

- Book of Choice
- Post It Notes
- Marker

## DIRECTIONS:

1. Before or after reading, have students choose a picture or illustration to identify the beginning sound. (Example:/t/ as in Tiger).
2. Write the letter on a Post It Note to add to the book.

**TIP** ALLOW YOUR CHILD TO WRITE THE LETTER USING A MARKER OF CHOICE TO PRACTICE LETTER FORMATION.

# BLOCK LETTER SOUNDS

## MATERIALS TO USE:

- Megablocks
- Stickers
- Expo Markers

## DIRECTIONS:

1. Choose between 2 and 4 letter sounds to practice.
2. Write the letter in a larger block using an expo marker.
3. Place stickers on singular blocks.
4. Place all the blocks out and allow the child to match the stickers to the letter.

**TIP** SAY THE NAME OUT LOUD OF EACH PICTURE BEFORE BEGINNING THE ACTIVITY TO HELP THE CHILD LISTEN TO THE INITIAL SOUND.

# LOST ANIMALS

## MATERIALS TO USE:

- Plastic Animals (or any toy)
- Paper

## DIRECTIONS:

1. Write the beginning letter sound of the animals on a piece of paper.
2. Tell your child that the animals are "lost"in the zoo  and they need to go back to their letter.
3. The child will say the name of the animal and identify the beginning sound.
4. Then, place the animal on the correct letter.

 TIP PAIR A BOOK THAT GOES WITH THE TOPIC TO BUILD THEIR BACKGROUND KNOWLEDGE.

# DOT A SOUND

## MATERIALS TO USE:

- Paper (A sketchbook is a great place to keep all these activities!)
- Stickers
- Dot Marker

## DIRECTIONS:

1. Choose between 2 and 4 letter sounds to practice. Tip: Include at least one short vowel.
2. Add the sticker the page with 2-3 letter options for each sticker.
3. Say the name of the sticker and then dot the letter that represents the correct beginning sound of the sticker.

## MODIFICATIONS:

- You can extend the activity to include sight words, blends, digraphs, and more!

 **TIP** HAVE YOUR CHILD CHOOSE THE STICKERS TO USE FOR THE ACTIVITY TO BOOST ENGAGEMENT AND OWNERSHIP OVER THEIR LEARNING.

# MAGNETIC LETTER MATCH

## MATERIALS TO USE:

- Cookie Sheet
- Expo Marker
- Magnetic Letters

## DIRECTIONS:

1. Write the letters of the alphabet on a cookie sheet using a dry erase marker.
2. Using magnetic letters match the letters.
3. While playing, talk to your child about each sound the letter represents.

## MODIFICATIONS:

- If all the letters are too overwhelming, work on letters they know first and add in a few more at a time.
- If your magnetic letters are lowercase, write the capital letter and have them match upper and lowercase letters.

 TIP ALLOW YOUR CHILD TO WRITE THE LETTER USING A MARKER OF CHOICE TO PRACTICE LETTER FORMATION.

# NAME KNOWLEDGE

## What is name knowledge?

Name knowledge is the ability to recognize and name the letters and their corresponding sounds in a child's name.

## Why is name knowledge important?

Research shows that one of the critical pieces of knowledge children should have by five is their own name -- to identify it, write it, and know it well. Children are also egocentric by nature and thus love learning about themselves. This is the first place we start when teaching letters!

## Keep in mind...

- This should be fun and exciting for your child. Their name is their identity and they will be proud to learn it.
- All kids learn at a different pace. Be patient with how fast they learn their name.

> Research has not determined any best order for teaching alphabet letters, but the one very definitive finding is an "own name advantage." They learn the letters in their own name first.
> (Justice, et al., 2006)

# BEST BOOKS FOR NAME KNOWLEDGE

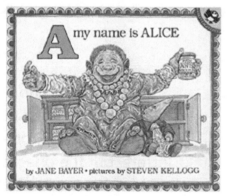

Include a personalized name book in your child's collection.

# LETTER MIX & FIX

## MATERIALS TO USE:

- magnetic letters (or wooden letters)
- Cookie Sheet (optional)

## DIRECTIONS:

1. Mix up the letters in your child's name
2. Allow them to "fix" the letters to spell their name.

## MODIFICATION:

- Write their name with an Expo Marker on the cookie sheet (or a sticky note next to it) for extra support.

TIP  HAVE YOUR CHILD SPELL OTHER NAMES OR WORDS THEY ARE CURIOUS ABOUT!

# LETTER DOT MATCH

 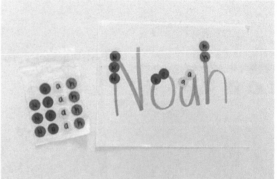

## MATERIALS TO USE:

- Dot Stickers
- Sharpie
- Paper

## DIRECTIONS:

1. Write your child's name on a piece of paper and each letter on the dot stickers.
2. Have your child match the dot sticker letter to the corresponding letter in their name.

## MODIFICATION:

- Place plain dot stickers on their name for fine motor practice.
- Have your child write their name and try it again!

 TIP  THIS IS AN EXCELLENT FINE MOTOR PRACTICE ACTIVITY AND GREAT FOR HAND STRENGTH.

# NAME KIT

## MATERIALS TO USE:

- Popsicle Sticks
- Magnetic Letters
- Construction Paper
- Marker/Crayon
- Ziploc Baggie

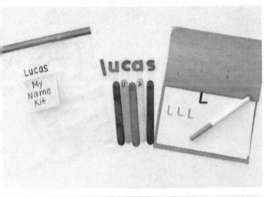

## DIRECTIONS:

1. Fill the bag with a personalized name book, magnetic letters, and popsicle stick letters.
2. Name Book - write each letter of their name on a page. On the last page, write their full name to practice putting it all together.
3. Other Items to add: letter stamps, colored pencils, stencils and play dough.

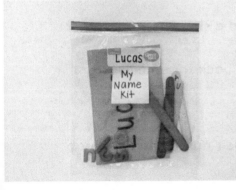

## MODIFICATIONS:

- Start small and add different materials as your child learns their name!

**TIP** THIS IS AN EASY ACTIVITY TO THROW IN YOUR BAG FOR RESTAURANTS OR TRAVEL!

# MEGABLOCK NAME

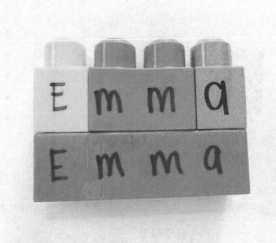

## MATERIALS TO USE:

- Dry Erase Marker
- Megablocks or Duplos

## DIRECTIONS:

1. Write their name on a longer block and then add a single letter to other blocks.
2. Children can match the letters to put the blocks back together.

## MODIFICATION:

- Have your child count the number of letters in their name and then grab that number of blocks to use.

 TIP THIS ACTIVITY ALSO BOOSTS FINE MOTOR SKILLS AND THE KINESTHETIC LEARNING IS AN ADDED BONUS!

# POST IT SCAVENGER HUNT

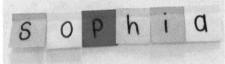

## MATERIALS TO USE:

- Post It Notes
- Marker

## DIRECTIONS:

1. Write each letter of your child's name on a sticky note.
2. Hide the sticky notes around the house for your child to search and find.
3. Once they've collected the letters they can put them together to spell their name!

## EXTENSION:

You can practice other words they are curious about!

**TIP** HAVE YOUR CHILD WRITE EACH LETTER ON THE STICKY NOTE TO PRACTICE THEIR WRITING SKILLS.

# LETTERS IN MY NAME

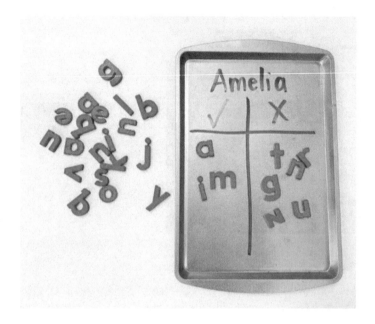

## MATERIALS TO USE:

- Cookie Sheet
- Magnetic Letters
- Dry Erase Markers

## DIRECTIONS:

1. Write your child's name at the top of the cookie sheet.
2. Under their name draw a T-Chart (shown above) with a check and an x.
3. Using a pile of magnetic letters, sort the letters by letters in their name (check side) and letters not in their name (x side).

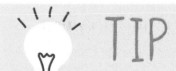 TIP ONCE THEY HAVE THEIR NAME DOWN, TEACH THEM HOW TO SPELL FAMILY MEMBERS' AND FRIENDS' NAMES!

# DOT ART NAME

## MATERIALS TO USE:

- Dot Markers
- Paper/Poster

## DIRECTIONS:

1. Write your child's name in marker on a piece of paper. You can also use craft paper to make it large or add it to a sketch book.
2. Let your child dot along the lines of each letter to create their name.

## EXTENSION:

- Let your child write their name with their favorite pen or marker!

 **TIP** ALLOW YOUR CHILD TO CHOOSE THE COLORS THEY USE FOR THE DOTS! THEIR CREATIVITY IS DEVELOPING, TOO!

# FIND THE MISSING LETTER

## MATERIALS TO USE:

- Cookie Sheet or Paper
- Magnetic Letters
- Expo Markers or Markers

## DIRECTIONS:

1. Write the child's name in expo marker (or regular marker) on the cookie sheet (or paper).
2. As you write their name, leave out a letters.
3. Add the missing letters using magnetic letters to complete each name.

## EXTENSION:

- Write in the missing letter using a marker or expo marker.
- As they become more proficient, leave out more than one letter.

TIP  LET THE CHILD PICK OUT THE MAGNETIC LETTERS IN THEIR NAME BEFORE THEY BEGIN.

# PLAYDOUGH NAME

## MATERIALS TO USE:

- Playdough
- Cookie Sheet or Tray (optional but contains the mess)

## DIRECTIONS:

1. Using play dough, the child will mold and shape each letter in their name.
2. Once they have shaped their name, try other letters, or names of people they know.

## EXTENSION:

- Using stamps or magnetic letters, the child can stamp their name in play dough.

# CREATE YOUR "NAMEBOW"

## MATERIALS TO USE:

- Paper or Sketchbook
- Markers
- Dot Stickers

## DIRECTIONS:

1. Write each letter of the child's name on a dot sticker.
2. The child will stick the letters in order of their name to create their "name bow!"

## EXTENSION:

- After they finish with the dot stickers, have them write their names in the different colors using markers.

 TIP WRITE THEIR NAME AT THE TOP IN THE SAME COLORS.

RHYMING

# RHYMING

## What is rhyming?

Rhyming is a word, a syllable or a line that has the same ending sound.

## Why is rhyming important?

Rhyming is one way children tune their ears to the sounds of language. Hearing the beginning sound, ending sound, similar and different sounds, are all ways children tune into the language and gain a stronger understanding of how letters, words, and reading are connected. Let's start with rhyming!

## Stages of Rhyming

Children learn to rhyme in three different stages:

- Exposure - Children are exposed to rhyming words through books, song and play.
- Hear & Recognize - Children begin to hear and are aware of when words do or do not rhyme.
- Rhyme Production - Children are able to add on to a rhyming word with one or multiple words.

> Rhyming ability is predictive of later reading achievement. (National Reading Panel, 2008)

# BEST BOOKS FOR RHYMING

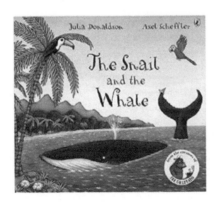

# PICTURE MATCH

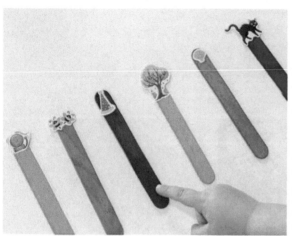 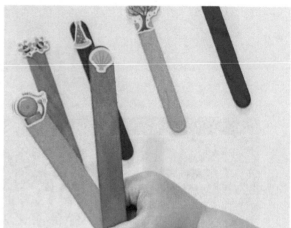

## MATERIALS TO USE:

- Stickers
- Marker
- Popsicle sticks

## DIRECTIONS:

1. Write each letter of your child's name on a sticky note.
2. Hide the sticky notes around the house for your child to search for.
3. Once they've collected the letters they can put them together to spell their name!

TIP ALLOW THE CHILD TO WRITE EACH LETTER ON THE STICKY NOTE TO PRACTICE THEIR WRITING SKILLS.

# RHYME TIME!

## MATERIALS TO USE:

- Muffin Tin
- Animal Figurines
- Tissue Paper
- Tape

## DIRECTIONS:

1. Fill a muffin tin with small objects (Safari LTD Toob animals are great for this!)
2. Cover the muffin tin with tissue paper or wrapping paper.
3. Pop each opening to pull out the hidden object and have your child think of 3-5 words that rhyme with it!

## EXTENSION

Have your child recall the initial letter sound and name the letter each object begins with.

**TIP** AFTER TRYING ONE ROUND, HAVE YOUR CHILD PICK THE NEXT 6 ITEMS TO WRAP UP!

# BUILD A RHYME

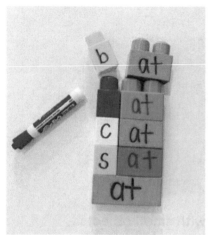  

## MATERIALS TO USE:

- Dry Erase Markers
- Megablock or Duplos

## DIRECTIONS:

1. Choose a base word to begin with or a common word family. Write that on a Megablock.
2. As your child thinks of words, add them to the blocks.
3. Have your child build the blocks together and practice reading the words together.

 **TIP** READ THROUGH THE RHYME BLOCKS WITH YOUR CHILD AFTER YOU MAKE THEM TOGETHER!

# WORD FAMILY FUN

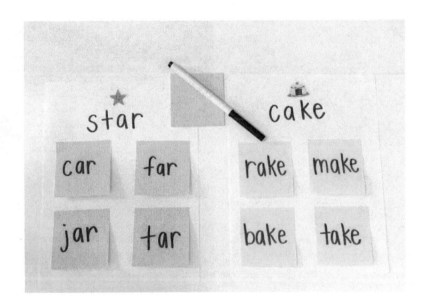

## MATERIALS TO USE:

- Stickers
- Post It Notes
- Marker
- Construction Paper

## DIRECTIONS:

1. Choose a picture or sticker to use as the base word and write the word on a piece of paper.
2. Ask your child to think of words that rhyme with the image.
3. Write each word on a post it note to make a fun anchor chart to hang up!

 TIP HIDE THE POST IT NOTES AROUND THE HOUSE TO MAKE A FUN SCAVENGER HUNT!

# SIDEWALK CHALK RHYMES

## MATERIALS TO USE:

- sidewalk chalk
- word family ideas
- open space outside

## DIRECTIONS:

1. Draw three boxes and a roof on the top box.
2. Write a word ending in the top triangle.
3. Model that ending sound.
4. Have your child hop and think of words that rhyme/end with that sound.

 **TIP** IF THEY AREN'T READY FOR RHYMING, ADD LETTERS TO PRACTICE SOUNDS.

# RHYME YOUR HEART OUT

## MATERIALS TO USE:

- Poetry
- Song Books
- Silly books

## DIRECTIONS:

1. Pull out your favorite poetry and song books.
2. Read and sing and dance while you notice all the rhyming!

## EXTENSION

Write your own songs to sing and dance to!

TIP SING FAVORITE SONGS LIKE "DOWN BY THE BAY" AND MAKE UP NEW AND SILLY VERSES.

# RHYME TOSS

## MATERIALS TO USE:

- Stickers
- Muffin Tin
- Pom Pom or small ball

## DIRECTIONS:

1. Place muffin liners in the muffin tin.
2. Add stickers to each muffin liner. Make sure they are pictures/stickers or words that they child will be able to rhyme.
3. Toss the pom pom into the muffin tin and say the name of the object/sticker then a rhyming word.

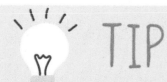 TIP LET YOUR CHILD THINK OF REAL WORDS AND NONSENSE WORDS TO MAKE IT FUN!

# RHYMING BASKET

FROG & DOG

TREE & TEA

## MATERIALS TO USE:

- Small Household Items or Toys
- Basket

## DIRECTIONS:

1. Grab a few household items that rhyme to add to the basket.
2. Match the items that rhyme.

## EXTENSION:

After they finish matching the items, see if they can go on a house hunt to find more items that rhyme!

 TIP USE ANYTHING YOU CAN FIND AROUND THE HOUSE - TOYS, KITCHEN ITEMS, HOME OFFICE SUPPLIES, AND MORE!

# BODY PART RHYME

EAR
FEAR
CHEER

## MATERIALS TO USE:

- Popsicle Stick - for a pointer

## DIRECTIONS:

1. Point to a part of the body (mouth, eyes, nose, knee, lips, thumb, cheek, head, hair, ear, etc.)
2. When they point to the body part, say the a word that rhymes. (Example: knee....bee!")

TIP ALWAYS MODEL A FEW EXAMPLES, FIRST! THIS HELPS YOUR CHILD UNDERSTAND AND HEAR THE RHYME.

# RHYME FREEZE TAG

## MATERIALS TO USE:

- 2 or more children

## DIRECTIONS:

1. The person who begins says a word. They will run and tag someone who will say a rhyming word.
2. If a child can not think of a rhyme, they are "frozen." They can become "unfrozen" when they are tagged again and can produce a rhyme.
3. When there are no more words to rhyme, the person who is "it" can think of another word to rhyme.

**TIP** CHILDREN CAN USE REAL AND NONSENSE WORDS DURING THIS GAME!

# PRE-WRITING SKILLS

# PRE-WRITING SKILLS

**What are pre-writing skills?**
Pre-writing is all the developmental, fine motor, and skill practice that leads up being able to write.

**Why is pre-writing important?**
We read aloud to kids for years before they can read on their own. There are MANY things we can do with kids to set them up for writing and fine motor success that start long before they begin to actually write. We want to give you fun and engaging ideas to do with your kids!

**Keep in mind...**
Every child will develop at their own pace, our job is to offer the opportunities for development to take place.

"Every drawing provides an opportunity to talk with a child, if that child is interested. In the process, language development is nurtured, knowledge is expanded, and narrative and expository skills are honed.

(Peterson, Jesso, & McCabe, 1999)

# PRE-WRITING SKILLS

Stages of Pre-Writing:

**10-24 MONTHS**

- Children begin to notice their ability to make marks and scribbles.
- Offer frequent mark-making opportunities.

**24-36 MONTHS**

- Around 2 the marks begin to have meaning to the child and they can express what they created.
- This parallels with the development of pretend play and imagination

**AGE 3**

- Writing begins to look more like writing.
- Drawings take clearer shape.
- Children begin to distinguish between drawing and writing.

**AGE 4**

- Children can write their own name.
- Children gain interest in words.
- Pictures become more detailed

**TIPS:**

- Always, always have your child interpret their writing and illustrations.
- Allow them the space to create, express themselves, make loads of mistakes, and grow!

# BEST BOOKS FOR PRE-WRITING SKILLS

Hazel Hutchins   Dušan Petričić

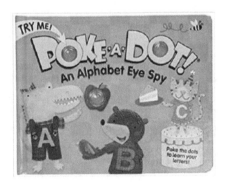

# PLAYDOUGH PLAY

## MATERIALS TO USE:

- Playdough or clay
- Stencils or utensils

## DIRECTIONS:

1. Get out playdough or clay.
2. Spend time playing with playdough, clay, or other molding materials to help develop hand strength.
3. Model how to create a few things and let the child free play, too!

## EXTENSION:

Use play dough to form letters.

**TIP** USE A PLASTIC KNIFE, FORK, OR KITCHEN TOOLS TO CREATE FUN DESIGNS.

# SORT IT OUT

## MATERIALS TO USE:

- colored Pom poms, beads, colored bears, or any small object
- Cups or containers

## DIRECTIONS:

1. Scoop, move or drop small objects (like pom poms) to a coordinating colors.
2. If they sort to the wrong color, you can talk through it with them, and model what to do.

## EXTENSION

Use magnatiles to create a container to keep the Pom poms in!

**TIP** MOVEMENT FROM LEFT TO RIGHT LAYS THE FOUNDATION FOR READING AND WRITING.

# LET'S SWIRL

 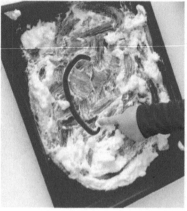 

## MATERIALS TO USE:

- shaving cream
- paint brush (optional)
- tray (to contain the mess)

## DIRECTIONS:

1. Fill tray with shaving cream and have your child create lines, shapes, letters or anything they feel inspired to draw!
2. To offer support, place letters or words on index cards to use as a model.

 **TIP** CHILDREN CAN PRACTICE SPELLING THEIR NAME OR ANY OTHER WORDS THEY ARE INTERESTED IN.

# Q-TIP PAINTING

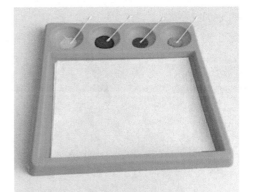

## MATERIALS TO USE:

- paper
- washable paint
- q-tips
- tray (optional)

## DIRECTIONS:

1. Use a Q-Tip to dip in washable paint to create shapes, lines, letters and pictures!
2. Let your child be creative and choose their paint colors and design!

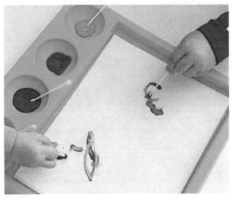

**TIP** USING A Q-TIP HELPS DEVELOP THEIR PINCHER GRASP WHICH IMPROVES HAND STRENGTH.

# SIDEWALK CHALK PAINTING

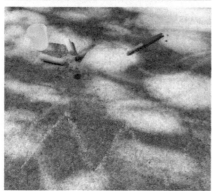

## MATERIALS TO USE:

- sidewalk chalk
- water
- paint brush

## DIRECTIONS:

1. Using side walk chalk, have your child draw lines, zigzags, dashes, or any design they would like!
2. Use a cup of water to dip a paint brush in to paint over the chalk line and watch it disappear!

TIP REMEMBER KIDS WATCH EVERYTHING - YOU MAY WANT TO MODEL AND DO IT WITH THEM!

# SIDEWALK CHALK PAINTING

## MATERIALS TO USE:

- corn starch
- water
- food coloring
- muffin tin
- paint brush

## DIRECTIONS:

1. Mix equal parts corn starch and water(2 cups is plenty for a muffin tin).
2. Divide mixture into a muffin tin.
3. Add 3-4 drops of food coloring to each muffin pocket. Mix well.
4. Use a paint brush to paint the driveway. It will dry a chalky and look beautiful!

 TIP  PAINT THEIR NAME OR LINES FOR THE CHILD TO TRACE.

# SPRAY BOTTLE PAINTING

## MATERIALS TO USE:

- Spray bottle
- Paper
- Painters Tape

## DIRECTIONS:

1. Mix 1/4 cup of water and 4-5 drops of food coloring in a spray bottle.
2. Place paper out for children to spray.
3. Use stencils to create an image.

 TIP USE A WHITE CRAYON TO DRAW A PICTURE OR WRITE A MESSAGE TO BE REVEALED WHEN THEY PAINT.

# LET'S DIG!

## MATERIALS TO USE:

- Regular or kinetic sand
- Shovels, kitchen utensils, or any other tool

## DIRECTIONS:

1. Create a sandy space for open play.
2. Allow your child to dig, move, and create.

This type of play builds hand strength and lets children practice manipulating their hands to do different things.

## EXTENSION

Add water for tougher digging and different types of play interactions.

 TIP ALLOW YOUR CHILD TO CHOOSE WHAT TOOLS AND TOYS THEY WANT TO PLAY WITH IN THE SAND!

# DOT MARKER CREATION

 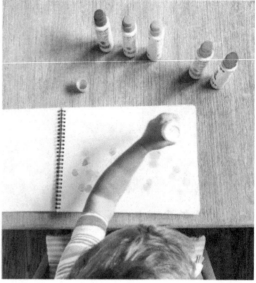

## MATERIALS TO USE:

- Dot markers
- paper

## DIRECTIONS:

1. Provide child with paper and an art space.
2. Show them how to take the lids on and off the markers (this is also great for hand strength.
3. Let them experience different types of mark-making with the markers.

## EXTENSION

Draw squiggles or lines and let them try to make marks on top of the lines!

 **TIP** YOU CAN MAKE A CREATION NEXT TO THEM SO THEY CAN SEE THE DIFFERENT THINGS TO TRY.

# FRUIT CUTTING

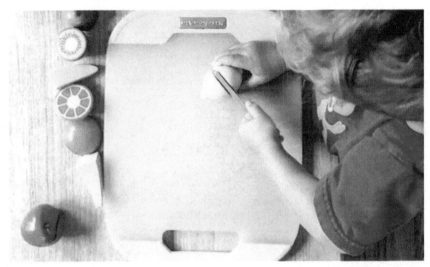

## MATERIALS TO USE:

- Real or pretend fruit
- Real or pretend knife

## DIRECTIONS:

1. Show the child how to cut the fruit with the knife.
2. Give them the knife and a piece of fruit.
3. Guide them in how to hold the knife to cut.

## EXTENSION

Allow them to do this with their fruit with most meals. They love the independence and the repeated practice is key!

This activity is particularly like writing because they have to hold something with one hand and manipulate something else with the other. It is so great for dexterity and strength, and of course, kids love it because they feel like a big kid doing it!

 TIP BE PATIENT AS THEY LEARN HOW TO HOLD THE KNIFE AND PUSH DOWN. IT IS HARDER THAN WE THINK!

# LET ME TAKE YOUR ORDER!

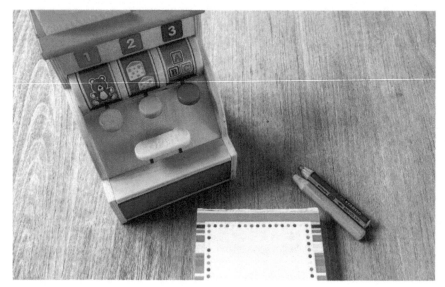

## MATERIALS TO USE:

- Washable utensil
- Small pad of paper
- Store or restaurant setup

## DIRECTIONS:

1. Set up a restaurant or store in their play space.  You can do this together!
2. Give them the paper and utensil.
3. Model how to take an order and let them write it down, no matter their level of writing.

## EXTENSION

Let them take orders at meal time or "write" the grocery list.

 TIP TRY NOT TO INTERVENE AND LET THEM TAKE OWNERSHIP OF THIS INTERACTION.

# MATH

## What is math?

Mathematics helps children make sense of the world around them and find meaning in the physical world. Through mathematics, children learn to understand their world in terms of numbers and shapes. They learn to reason, to connect ideas, and to think logically (Where Learning Begins, 1999).

## Why is math important?

We both have enough classroom and kid experience to know the importance of math in the early years. We wanted to share with you a few fun activities you can do with your child to learn foundational math skills through reading and play!

## Keep in mind...

Hands-on math experience is best. The more children interact with their world, the better.

Both males and females, mathematical precocity early in life predicts later creative contributions and leadership in critical occupational roles.
(Lubinski, Benbow, & Kell, 2014)

# COLORS

## MATERIALS TO USE:

- Pouch tops
- Peg board
- Other colored pieces

## DIRECTIONS:

1. Use a simple picture.
2. Match the colored pieces to create the picture.
3. You can also use peg board found on Amazon.

**TIP** PAIRING BOOK WITH A MATHEMATICAL TOPIC IS A GREAT WAY TO REINFORCE CONCEPTS.

# MIXING COLORS

## MATERIALS TO USE:

- Washable Paint
- Paper
- Easle (optional)

## DIRECTIONS:

1. Read "Mix It Up" and talk about the different colors.
2. Show your child the paint colors and add them to the paint tray (we love using ice cube trays).
3. Allow your child to use the color to paint.
4. Add another color as they continue painting.

 TIP THEY CAN PAINT WITH THEIR FINGERS, BRUSHES, Q-TIPS OR PLASTIC SILVERWARE.

# ROLL & DOT COUNTING

## MATERIALS TO USE:

- Dice
- Dot Marker

## DIRECTIONS:

1. Roll the dice and count the number of dots.
2. Find the matching number on the paper and use the dot markers to make the same number of dice.
3. OPTIONAL - Use two die or roll the dice twice for numbers greater than 6.

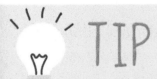 TIP  HAVE THE CHILD TOUCH EACH CIRCLE AS THEY COUNT TO PRACTICE 1:1 CORRESPONDENCE.

# EDIBLE COUNTING

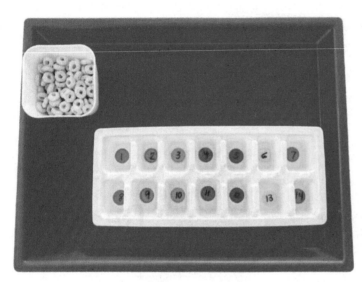

## MATERIALS TO USE:

- Muffin Tin, Ice Tray - anything that separates small items
- Cheerios, Chocolate chips or goldfish
- Sticker Dots

## DIRECTIONS:

- Write numbers 1-10 on dot stickers
- Place the number of cheerios to match the digit.
- EAT when they are finished counting!

 TIP TRY TO THINK WHAT YOU CAN PUT IN YOUR YARD THAT CAN BE HANDS ON FOR YOUR CHILD.

# MEASURING

## MATERIALS TO USE:

- Measuring Cups
- Water
- Food Coloring

## DIRECTIONS:

1. Fill water bottles with water and a little food coloring.
2. Allow your child to explore pouring the liquid into measuring cups, spoons and large mixing bowls.

 TIP    ADD A LINE TO THE BOWL OR CUP TO HAVE THE CHILD MEASURE TO THE LINE.

# MORE MEASURING

## MATERIALS TO USE:

- Mixing Bowls
- Measuring Cups
- Measuring Spoons
- Recipe Ingredients

## DIRECTIONS:

One of the best learning experiences that tie in both math and science is cooking or baking with your child! Grab your favorite recipe and have fun together in the kitchen!

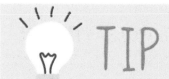 **TIP** DON'T BE AFRAID TO LET IT GET A LITTLE MESSY! CLEANING UP IS A GREAT LIFE SKILL TO TACK ON!

# LENGTH MEASURING

## MATERIALS TO USE:

- tape measure
- ruler
- yardstick

## DIRECTIONS:

Kids love to mimic what they see. Include them on a household project and allow them to try out the tools. A tape measure is perfect for kids! Show them how to use it and teach them what it means when they measure something. Compare two things like books shown here.

TIP · HAVE THEM SELECT THE ITEMS THEY WANT TO MEASURE AND COMPARE!

# SHAPE MATCH GAME

## MATERIALS TO USE:

- Post It Notes
- Paper Plates (or paper)
- Markers

## DIRECTIONS:

1. Draw and label a paper plate with a shape.
2. Draw one shape on each post it note.
3. Place post it notes around the house or in a bin to pull out.
4. Match the shape on the post it note with the shape on the paper plate.

**TIPS** COLOR COORDINATE THE SHAPES WITH A COLOR TO HELP CHILDREN IDENTIFY COLORS, TOO!

# SHAPE PUZZLE

My Very
First Book of
**Shapes**

by Eric Carle

## MATERIALS TO USE:

- Shape Sorter

## DIRECTIONS:

1. Using the shape blocks have the child match the shape block to their cut out.
2. Help child identify and match the shapes as they sort them!

 TIP SHAPE PUZZLES ALSO MAKE A GREAT LEARNING ACTIVITY!

# SIZE

## MATERIALS TO USE:

- Lego Duplos or Megablocks

## DIRECTIONS:

1. Create a tower.
2. Have child create the same tower with another color block, but add one more.
3. Continue until they have built multiple towers.
4. Place the towers next to each other so the child can see the difference.
5. Count each block in the tower.

TIPS SORTING EACH TOWER BY COLOR MAKES A GREAT WAY TO TEACH COLORS, TOO!

# BIG, MEDIUM, SMALL

## MATERIALS TO USE:

- Figurines
- Cardboard box (or any paper/poster board can work)

## DIRECTIONS:

1. Give child a group of figurines (or any items to sort).
2. Model how to compare each figurine and place into either the "big, medium. or small" category.
3. Sort the figurines.

TIP WHEN YOU WRITE THE LABELS FOR EACH CATEGORY, WRITE THE TITLE BASED ON SIZE.

# SORTING

## MATERIALS TO USE:

- Counting Bears
- Colored Paper

## DIRECTIONS:

1. Choose a category with items to sort. We suggest starting with colors.
2. Using counting bears (pom poms, construction paper, small toys).
3. Sort the objects by placing them in the correct categories.
4. As they are sorting, discuss with them what you are noticing.

 TIP CATEGORIES FOR SORTING: LETTERS/NUMBERS, TYPES OF FOOD (FRUIT, VEGETABLE), COLORS, VEHICLES, HABITATS.

# MORE SORTING

## MATERIALS TO USE:

- Figurines
- Labels (land, air, water)

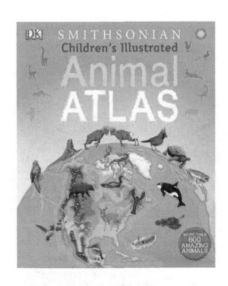

## DIRECTIONS:

1. Provide children with figurines (animals or transportation figurines work great for sorting land, air and water).
2. Have the child decide which item belongs in each category.

 TIP WHEN THEY HAVE COMPLETED THE ACTIVITY, HAVE THE CHILD EXPLAIN THEIR REASONING FOR PLACING EACH ITEM IN THE CATEGORY.

# LIFE SKILLS

**What are life skills?**

Life skills can range from social-emotional behaviors (taking turns and awareness of others) to physical behaviors (using scissors).

**Why are life skills important?**

Life skills are important because it effects HOW children learn in the classroom setting. When life skills have been mastered, teachers and parents can spend more time on developing social emotional skills and academic skills. Research is finding that Social Emotional Learning has a significant impact on achievement and teaching those skills early matters!

**Keep in mind...**

Children can learn so much from their peers! If your child is struggling with a life skill, sometimes a little help from a friend is all they need.

Kids who took part in SEL-informed curricula saw an 11% jump in academic achievement compared to those who did not participate. (CASEL Report, 2011)

# PHYSICAL SKILLS

Many of the physical skills that can help children navigate the world of kindergarten can be practiced beginning in early toddlerhood. These are skills that parents and caregivers work on daily with their children to help develop their motor skills and growing independence. As we mentioned earlier in the book, follow your child's lead. If they are showing interest in a skill, help to nurture that skill, and be patient!

- Tying shoes
- Using scissors
- Opening lunch box and wrappers
- Zipping and buttoning clothing
- Holding a pencil or crayon
- Using the restroom independently (flush/wash)
- Washing Hands

# COMMUNICATION SKILLS

Being able to communicate with children is a skill that parents begin in infancy with nonverbal cues, sign language and gestures, speaking one and two word phrases.  This goes all the way into preschool and early kindergarten when children are able to communicate complete thoughts. When children enter kindergarten, even the most outgoing children can exhibit shyness and nervousness. So, if on the first day of kindergarten your normally outgoing five year old is unable to speak in complete sentences, give them time to adjust.

- Asking for help
- Responding to their name
- Speaking in complete sentences
- Asking or answering a question
- Make meal choices (breakfast and lunch)
- Follow multi-step directions
- Listen and react to a read aloud
- Knowing their address and phone number

# SOCIAL EMOTIONAL SKILLS

Social Emotional abilities are a large part of a child's success in kindergarten. Social emotional learning is the process of acquiring and applying the knowledge necessary to manage and understand emotions, set goals, establish and maintain a relationship, and show and feel empathy (Every Student Succeeds Act, 2015). Most of these skills are learned and practiced daily before, during, and after their kindergarten year. Reading picture books that model social emotional skills is a great way to introduce and teach these skills to children. We read these stories from the beginning and as children get older, you can have more conversations about these skills.

- Shares and takes turns with others
- Solve a problem (with or without adult intervention)
- Continues with a difficult task
- Engages in cooperative play
- Identifies some emotions (in themselves and others)
- Making friends
- Calm down when upset

# REFERENCES

Atwell, M.N. & Bridgeland, J.M. (2019). Ready to Lead: A 2019 Update of Principals' Perspectives on How Social and Emotional Learning Can Prepare Children and Transform Schools. A Report for Collaborative for Academic, Social, and Emotional Learning.

Baker, C. E., Vernon-Feagans, L., & The Family Life Project Investigators. (2015). Fathers' language input during shared book activities: Links to children's kindergarten achievement. Journal of Applied Developmental Psychology, 36, 53–59.

Cuffaro, H. K. (1995). Experimenting with the world: John Dewey and the early childhood classroom. New York, NY: Teachers College Press.

Eliot, L. (1999). What's Going on in There? : How the Brain and Mind Develop in the First Five Years of Life. Bantam Books.

Hammill, D. D. (2004). What We Know about Correlates of Reading. Exceptional Children, 70(4), 453–469. https://doi.org/10.1177/001440290407000405

Harris, L. (2003). An assessment of the impact of First Book's northeast program.

Justice, L.M., Pence, K., Bowles, R., & Wiggins, A.K. (2006). An Investigation of the Four Hypothesis Concerning the Order by Which 4-Year-Old Children Learn the Alphabet Letters." Early Childhood Research Quarterly 21 (3): 374-89.

Lester, S. and Russell, W. (2008). Play for a Change: Play, Policy and Practice - a Review of Contemporary
Perspectives. London: National Children's Bureau.

Lubinski, D., Benbow, C. P., & Kell, H. J. (2014). Life Paths and Accomplishments of Mathematically Precocious Males and Females Four Decades Later. Psychological Science, 25(12), 2217–2232.

# REFERENCES

McNamara, D & Neufeld, G. (2016). Rest, Play, Grow: Making Sense of Preschoolers (Or Anyone Who Acts Like One). Aona books.

National Academy of Education., & Anderson, R. C. (1985). Becoming a nation of readers: The report of the Commission on Reading. Washington, D.C: National Academy of Education.

National Early Literacy Panel. (2008). Developing early literacy: Report of the National Early Literacy Panel. Washington, DC: National Institute for Literacy.

O'Leary, W. (2021). Play-Based Learning: What It Is and Why It Should Be a Part of Every Classroom. https://blog.edmentum.com/play-based-learning-what-it-and-why-it-should-be-part-every-classroom

Parten, M (1932). "Social participation among preschool children". Journal of Abnormal and Social Psychology 28 (3): 136–147.

Peterson, C.L., Jesso, B., & McCabe, A. (1999). Encouraging narratives in preschoolers: An intervention study. Journal of Child Language, 26(1): 49-97.

Snow, K. L. (2006). Measuring school readiness: conceptual and practical considerations. Early Educ. Dev. 17, 7–41. doi: 10.1207/s15566935eed1701_2

UNICEF (2018). Learning Through Play: Strengthening Learning Through Play in Early Childhood Programs.

# THANK YOU!

Thank you for your purchase! We are truly grateful for your support and purchasing this resource. We hope this book makes a difference in your home and time you spend with your child. If you have any questions, concerns, suggestions, or requests, please email us at kreadythroughplay@gmail.com. We are always happy to help and want to encourage a love of learning!

-Becca & Sarah

# TERMS OF USE

You may use this for personal/student use in a single classroom or home. Please do not give or copy this item for others, share on a website, or post this item or its contents for sale. All contents of this PDF is copyrighted material. Thank you and enjoy it for years to come!

# FOLLOW BECCA & SARAH

Click the icons to check out our websites, social media and Teachers Pay Teachers shops for all of our latest resources and tips!

## BECCA'S BOOK BOX

## WONDERFULLY READ

Made in the USA
Coppell, TX
01 March 2022

74233681R10083